things a man
should never do past 30

Esquire

things
a man
should
never
do past

David Katz

30

Hearst Books
A Division of Sterling Publishing Co., Inc.
New York

Copyright © 2005 by Hearst Communications, Inc.

Designed by Pauline Neuwirth, Neuwirth & Associates, Inc.

Library of Congress Cataloging-in-Publication Data
Katz, David, 1975-
  Esquire things a man should never do past thirty / David Katz.
      p. cm.
  Includes bibliographical references and index.
  ISBN 1-58816-469-1 (alk. paper)
  1. Middle aged men--Humor. 2. Men--Humor. I. Title: Things a man should
never do past thirty. II. Title.
  PN6231.M47K37 2005
  818'.602--dc22

                                                    2005012343

10 9 8 7 6 5 4 3 2

Published by Hearst Books
A Division of Sterling Publishing Co., Inc.
387 Park Avenue South, New York, NY 10016

Esquire is a registered trademark of Hearst Communications, Inc.

www.esquire.com

For information about custom editions, special sales, premium and corporate
purchases, please contact Sterling Special Sales Department at 800-805-5489
or specialsales@sterlingpub.com.

Distributed in Canada by Sterling Publishing
c/o Canadian Manda Group, 165 Dufferin Street
Toronto, Ontario, Canada M6K 3H6

Distributed in Australia by Capricorn Link (Australia) Pty. Ltd.
P.O. Box 704, Windsor, NSW 2756 Australia

Printed in USA

ISBN 1-58816-469-1

contributors

Tyler Cabot

Doug Cantor

Matt Haber

Brian Frazer

Stacy Grenrock Woods

A.J. Jacobs

Doug Lansky

Rachel Lehmann-Haupt

Peter Martin

Robert Miles

Ashley Phillips

Sara Reistad-Long

Mike Sacks

Adam Sank

Penny Wrenn

things a man
should never do past 30

See any movie with elves, mutants, wookies, or other non-human characters on opening night.

Use the word *party* as a verb.

Pre-party.

Wear ironic baseball caps (John Deere, CAT) unless he actually operates heavy machinery for a living.

Drink Ironic beer (Rheingold, Schlitz) unless he actually likes it.

**Make an ass-related pun about
the colon or semicolon.**

Make inane inside jokes on
Evite message boards (e.g., "Yo
McFloozy, don't forget to bring
Liz's fuzzy wonder!")

**Eat or drink anything with the word
"X-TREME!" on the label.**

Use sports metaphors
for sex, as in, "Rita
and I are ready to
start a family, so she
pulled the goalie."

Use sex metaphors for sports.

Use a bottle opener
for his key chain.

**Use more than one
exclamation point
in a row.**

Mix fountain sodas.

Figure out which dirty
words are spelled by
his phone number.

Have an emotional attachment to Lara Croft.

Put a bra on his head— for any reason.

Call in sick because of a hangover.

TiVo *Stacked*.

High five in a business situation.

Stick anything (e.g., Wiffle bat, large branch) between his legs for comedic effect.

Request an autograph.

Own more than two halogen lamps.

Quote *Office Space*, *Swingers*, or *Old School* more than once in a week.

Watch *Dancing with the Stars*.

Audition for *The Biggest Loser*.

Mosh.

Poetry-slam.

Instant
Message.

Flash the hang-loose hand sign, even if he is actually hanging loose.

Refer to oral sex as "going south with the mouth."

Get the news from Jimmy Kimmel.

Wake up on his neighbor's lawn, minus his pants, again.

Refer to unprotected sex as "the old pull and pray."

things a man past 30 SHOULD NOT DO IN THE COMPANY OF WOMEN

Point out another womans's breasts, or compare them to ours, even favorably.

> *Drink red wine with a straw, even if he's just gotten his teeth bleached.*

Pretend he knows what's wrong with our iPod.

> *Say he can drive a stick when he can't.*

Be more indecisive than we are.

> *If someone cuts him off while driving, roll down the window and spit at the car's window.*

Laugh too hard at his own jokes.

> *Ignore female friends; ours, or his.*

Feel that his purpose in life is to always play the devil's advocate.

> *Be a picky eater or an obsessive hand-washer.*

High five us or call us "man."

> *When the check comes, say, "Are you gonna help me with this?"*

Call his mother for a second opinion.

> *After sex, do a play-by-play or leave the condom on the floor.*

things a man past 30 SHOULD NOT
DO IN THE COMPANY OF WOMEN

Imitate bodily functions.

Slick his hair back.

Grope at the movies.

Say we look like his mother, sister, or any other relative with whom offspring could display birth defects.

Say "I like a woman who…"

Eat more candy than we do.

Pull rank, beg, or slip a fifty to a nightclub bouncer.

Quake at the thought of purchasing or carrying tampon boxes, purses, etc.

Ask if we have had plastic surgery.

Order the most expensive wine on the list unless he knows how to pronounce it.

Play the "who's your daddy?" card.

Anything he did when he was 19.

Rachel Lehmann-Haupt

Sara Reistad-Long

Refer to breasts as "fun bags."

**Refer to his penis as
"Sir Phillip Wagstaff."**

Refer to attractive
mothers as "MILFS."

Wear flip flops to
an office function.

Marvel at the acerbic wit
of David Spade.

Nickel slots.

Own a novelty pet
(especially an iguana).

**Listen to
Widespread Panic.**

Travel to attend a
String Cheese Incident concert.

**Make his pet drink alcoholic
beverages or blow bong
smoke into its mouth.**

Accidentally pee anywhere.

Jell-O shots.

Body shots.

Do impressions of Austin Powers
characters, especially Dr. Evil.

Crash on a friend's floor.

Experiment with facial hair.

Let his underpants show above his jeans or below his shorts.

Own beer-drinking paraphernalia.

Ask friends to help him move.

Apply paint to his face for any reason at all.

Own a skull bong.

Know the names of the current *Real World* cast.

Bring his mitt to a professional baseball game.

Use Dial soap as shampoo.

Purchase *House of Wax* on DVD.

Yell, "Run, Forrest, Run!" at someone in the airport trying to catch his plane.

Eat cereal endorsed by a cartoon character.

Eat raw hamburger meat, telling himself it's basically steak tartare.

Try to fart, burp, and sneeze all at the same time.

Camp out for concert tickets.

Channel Frank the Tank.

Use the word *sexcellent*.

Put his face between a woman's breasts and make a gurgling motorboat sound.

Believe that that is in fact the stripper's real name, college, or hometown.

Use a "crunk" song for his cell-phone ring.

Googlewack.

Bet it all on black.

Bet it all on red.

Arm wrestle in public.

Open a beer with
anything other than
a bottle opener.

Hang anything from
the rearview mirror.

Lightly bang fists when a
handshake will suffice.

Refer to his testicles as "Chang and Eng."

Devise secret
handshakes.

Mix Kool-Aid with hard liquor.

Call in to *American Idol*.

Use a wallet that is fastened with Velcro.

Refer to Latina women as *mamasitas*.

Dry hump.

Have a welcome mat in front of his home that says, FUCK OFF.

Sport an ironic mustache.

Watch Japanimation in his underwear.

Practice his autograph.

**Watch past the end credits
for the Adam Sandler "gag reel."**

Scream like a woman.

Act like a child.

Cry like a baby.

Kiss his biceps and
refer to them as "guns"
or "pythons."

Rank his friends in order of
"best," "second best," and so on.

Travel to Amsterdam
for no other reason than
the really good weed.

Use cologne as a
room deodorizer.

Hacky Sack.

Have a novelty answering-machine message.

Use a large cardboard
box as a coffee table.

Drink Long Island iced teas.

Own "china" emblazoned
with the logo of a professional
sports franchise.

Beer-bong.

Teach foreign speakers that the
way to ask directions in English is
"Will you tickle my man snake?"

**Keep a regularly updated,
running tally of his sex partners.**

Jump and knock chests
with a coworker.

Wear swim trunks as an
underwear substitute.

**Model his life and
hairstyle after
The Cure's Robert Smith.**

**The deep satisfaction
of wearing an employee-
of-the-month hat.**

The subscription number for
Mel Gibson's father's newsletter.

**Colin Farrell's
zodiac sign.**

The current highest-scoring
WNBA player.

The current highest-scoring
SlamBall player.

**What bonus material is
included on the DVD of *Hitch*.**

The electric slide.

Where to buy a really good ascot.

Any of the words
to Avril Lavigne's
"Sk8er Boi."

The ingredients of a ballpark frank.

Rosie O'Donnell.

His mother's preferred
sexual positions.

Which Culkin brother has the creamiest skin.

A good price on Vagisil.

How to say "Show us your tits" in Pashto.

The secret location of the mother ship, which shall ferry the faithful to the planet Bozon.

Exciting recent breakthroughs in aromatherapy.

The taste of his own toenails.

How to zest up an
otherwise vapid fondue.

**The tour schedule for
Steve Miller.**

Refer to his friends, or his testes, as "my boys."

Drink beer out of a helmet.

Reiterate how much he puked last night.

Wear a T-shirt with a rhino on it that says, "I'm horny."

**Name his penis his name
plus the word *junior*.**

Own a beanbag chair.

Use the word dawg in a
sentence when not referring
to a Canine.

Own a futon.

Hang art with tape.

Hang "Starry Night" or "The Scream" on his wall— unless he paid more than 20 million for them.

Drink malternative beverages.

Don a puka-bead necklace.

Break up with a girlfriend by e-mail.

Engage in pranks
involving airborne food.

Own a Lava lamp.

Pool hop.

Live with someone
you aren't sleeping with
or did not father.

Share a hotel room with
someone you aren't sleeping with
or did not father.

Play fantasy sports.

Divide a restaurant bill with a friend in any way other than 50-50.

Sleep past noon.

Mention his SAT score without specifically being asked about it. And even then he should at least appear to strain to recollect what it was.

Cook exclusively on a
George Foreman grill.

Wear a jersey with the name of a
professional athlete on the back.

Refer to a woman's genitalia as her "nappy dugout."

Employ any other
pickup line besides
"Hi, my name is ___.
What's yours?"

Use Internet acronyms, especially ROFL and LOL.

Shave any part of your body except your face.

Attend Mardi Gras, Carnaval, or Burning Man.

Own a fish tank.

Lure women back to his home with the promise of checking out said fish tank.

Enjoy Michael Bay movies.

Fall asleep in public.

Call drugs by their street names (e.g., smack, crank, rock).

Pick a fistfight by thrusting out his neck, flexing, and screaming, "It's go time!"

items a man past the age of 30
SHOULD NOT OWN

A home brewing kit.

A Gilbert Godfried comedy album.

A beer funnel.

A case for high school sports trophies.

Inflatable furniture.

A BB gun.

A Donald Trump Bobble head doll.

A poster featuring an X Games athlete.

A Sports Illustrated *football phone.*

Snowboarding videos.

Season 2 of the World Poker Tour on DVD.

Blacklight posters.

An "I Brake for Hooters" bumper sticker.

A Boa constrictor.

items a man past the age of 30
SHOULD NOT OWN

*A Lamborghini poster. A Lamborghini model.
A Lamborghini calendar. A Lamborghini.*

The Wrestlemania 21 program.

The Girls of the Big 12 calendar.

An "Official Bikini Inspector" hat.

A foam "shocker" hand.

[Commemorative or Collectible] State spoons.

A Hard Rock Café T-Shirt.

Stolen street signs.

*Beer cozies that read "I'm not as think as you drunk
I am."*

An ICBM.

A Che Guevara T-Shirt.

A portable gaming device.

*Eva Longoria's cheerleading outfit, as purchased on
eBay.*

Eat cottage cheese.

Get a personalized license plate–unless your state will permit tags that read ASSHOLE.

Date a superior.

Date a subordinate.

Date a stripper.

Ask a policeman, "You ever shoot anybody with that thing?"

Ask a woman, "Hey, you got a license for that ass?"

Skip.

Install carpet over hardwood.

Take a camera to a nude beach.

Wear a Speedo unless he is a world-class swimmer and is actually about to race.

Enjoy any type of entertainment hosted by Johnny Mosley.

Force or be forced to drink anything.

Let his father do his taxes.

Order Italian food in a
non-Italian restaurant.

Order chardonnay in a dive bar.

Drink Tequiza.

Buy a watch on the sidewalk.

Smile at a mime.

Bowl with sober people.

Bowl to techno music.

Use the sentence
"Don't you know who I am?"

Feed the animals.

Tap on the glass.

Devote his life to the credos spelled out in Jimmy Buffett's "Cheeseburger in Paradise."

Drink and drive the lawn mower.

"Pimp out" a work cubicle.

Own a strobe light.

**Take the lead
in a conga line.**

Refer to breasts as
"chesticles."

Purchase gag condoms.

**Shout out a response to:
"Are you ready to rock?"**

Purchase flavored
popcorn by the tub.

**Decorate a bedroom with
promotional liquor freebies.**

.

Feed his dog from his mouth.

Feed his girlfriend from his mouth.

How to say anything in Klingon.

How to say anything in Elvish.

What Britney Spears's head looks like when pasted onto somebody else's naked body.

Where to buy an "authentic" bolo tie.

things a man should NOT know
(AT ANY AGE)

**The difference between a
double axel and a triple lutz.**

The details of his wife's first
sexual encounter.

A vegan.

The date on which the
Hilary Duff became legal.

**The sassiest thing
Star Jones said today
on *The View*.**

That Kelly Ripa
has a book club.

Cher's real age.

The names of the
American Idol finalists.

His best friend's salary.

**The latest book in Kelly Ripa's
book club.**

Tobey Maguire's middle name.

The placement of *While You Were Sleeping* on E!'s "Rank: 25 Best Date Movies."

That the female long-eared groundhog is an animal likely to engage in lesbian behavior, including complicated acts of oral sex.

Use the word "collated" on a resume.

Sleep in the empty bathtub of a Las Vegas hotel room.

Refer to a 40-ounce bottle of malt liquor as "a beer."

Leave *American Pie 3* or *Matrix Reloaded* in his DVD carousel for more than two days.

Use an emoticon
in an e-mail.

**Hold a weekly "house meeting"
with roommates.**

Burp out
pithy sayings.

Eat tuna straight
from the can.

Steal from his father.

Use body parts as surrogate ventriloquist dummies.

Lie to his mother.

Flip to the "B-Side" of his underwear.

Use photos of former frat bros as screen savers.

Breathlessly follow Top 40 radio countdowns.

Name pets after Middle Earth creatures.

Categorize his liquor collection on an ascending "getting fucked up" scale.

Reality shows that feature a hot tub and/or pool table.

Any movie that ends at the prom.

Napoleon Dynamite.

Those HBO shows with fat people who have balloon fetishes.

Any show or movie with Xtreme in the title.

Taxicab confessions.

Sabado Gigante while stoned.

E!

Movies based on a *Saturday Night Live* character.

One Tree Hill.

Rockumentaries.

National Lampoon's anything.

Battling robots.

Freddie Prinze Jr.

Sequels after No. 3, unless they star Jenna Jameson,

Any show that has ever aired on the WB, ever.

Shows featuring the words "When" and "Attack" in the title.

MTV.

Baywatch 1993-96, '98.

Saved by the Bell reruns.

Shows with competitive plastic surgery.

The World's Strongest Man Competition on ESPN 2.

High school cheerleading championships on ESPN 2.

ESPN 2.

Any type of wrestling except that does not involve
mud or Jell-O.

Anime porn.

Anything with deuce or bigelow in the title.

Flash gang-signs while posing for wedding photos.

Fire up a "Dutch oven."

Use cologne anywhere below the belt.

Collect book-length volumes of newspaper funnies.

Give "shout outs."

Celebrate special occasions
at establishments featuring
animatronic animals.

**Masturbate to scenarios
involving the girls from
The O.C.**

Bring his "game face"
anywhere.

Consider AC/DC's
"Big Balls" his song.

Tie a bandanna
around his wrist.

Combine bubblegum flavors.

Shave superhero logos
into his scalp.

Raise hermit crabs.

Make love to the accompaniment of disaster-movie soundtracks.

Color-coordinate bandanas for him and his dog.

Hug amusement park characters.

Sniff glue.

things a man should
NOT DO IN BED PAST 30

1. Play drums on his partner's ass.

2. Squeal.

3. Use the word "smokin' " unless he's actually smoking.

4. Smoke.

5. Compare.

6. Whinny.

7. Call it his "schlong."

8. Be silent.

9. Be boring.

10. Time his climax to Roxy Music's "Avalon."

11. Use a device called anything like "Jenna's Realistic Pussy and Ass."

12. Liken his partner's body to "a wonderland."

13. Lubricate with cooking oil.

14. Start a sentence: "In the future."

15. Put his index fingers on either side of his head, indicating a bull.

16. Even mention jazz.

17. Anything with rose petals.

18. Talk about electronics.

19. Pout.

20. Use the phrase "fyi."

21. Request a rim job.

22. Reuse a condom.

23. Light incense.

24. Emulate Jim Morrison.

25. Whine.

26. Recite verse.

27. Consider his bed "where the magic happens."

28. Beg.

Stacy Grenrock Woods

Own the *Dodgeball* movie poster.

Eat the worm.

Seriously train for an eating contest.

Get pirated cable and brag about it.

Write song parodies
and leave them on his
answering machine.

**Write song parodies and
leave them on other people's
answering machines.**

Play tetherball.

Form a
cover band.

Wake up to a "morning zoo."

Wear anything tie-dyed.

Have sideburns larger than his hand.

Blow a bubble, unless it's to amuse a kid.

Look up any dirty word
in the dictionary.

Xerox his ass.

Wear Disney-themed neckties.

Act pissed if he gets carded.

**Doodle heavy-metal band
logos.**

Boogie board.

Brag to colleagues about the size and circumference of his bowel movements.

Check out the "bonus features" on a Vin Diesel DVD.

Compare the trajectory of his life with those of the characters in Billy Joel's "Scenes from an Italian Restaurant."

Design his ultimate graffiti tag.

Memorize professional wrestling stats.

Request extra sprinkles.

Spit for show.

"Air drum."

Weave and/or distribute
friendship bracelets.

Choose "69" as his jersey number.

Customize bank checks
with NFL emblems.

Eat Oreo cookies in stages.

Coin his
own nickname.

Volunteer to be a
magician's assistant.

Brag about
how much
he can bench.

**Live in his parents' basement
or attic.**

Eat any food products
made by Chef Boyardee.

The chicken dance.

**His favorite
Bizzarro comic.**

How to make one
mean ambrosia salad.

Where to pick up the perfect
inspirational desk calendar.

**Wilmer Valderrama's
filmography.**

Killer scrapbooking techniques.

How to mix a slippery nipple, a screaming orgasm, or a sloe comfortable screw.

How to carve tofurkey.

A single lyric from any song ever sung by O-Town.

A fair price for a pedicure.

The slugging percentage of that journeyman left fielder whom the Braves just traded to the Rockies and who may be a nice pickup for his fantasy baseball team.

What it is like to walk around the city wearing a velvet cloak.

The melody to the theme song from the show "Charmed."

His local priest's boxer or brief predilection.

The name of Rue McClanahan's character on *The Golden Girls*.

What happens to the little cows before they become the delicious veal on his plate.

More than two lines from the film *Fletch 2*.

How to play a James Taylor song on the guitar.

Any 900 number by heart.

How to order a
mail-order bride.

His bra-cup size.

The current cast members
of *Movin' Out!*

**His parents' favorite
sexual position.**

How to manufacture napalm.

What it sounds like if he puts a microphone in front of a megaphone.

How to cross-stitch.

The cost of a pair of chaps.

What was in the final issue of *Rosie* magazine.

Describe in vivid and specific detail how a public restroom smells.

Cheer drunken brawls.

Subscribe to the Victoria's Secret catalogue.

Giggle whenever
someone brings up
the penal system.

Vomit in public.

Go commando.

Sleep on a bare mattress.

End a conversation by saying "lates."

Display posters of
Pamela Anderson
in his home.

Hold his lighter up at a concert.

Host a kegger.

**Wear a tank top anywhere
but to the gym.**

Wear Designer Imposters body spray.

Publicly greet friends by shouting,"What's up, you whore?"

Don a faux-hawk.

Listen to Van Halen (regardless of lead singer).

Party at his parents' home while they're away.

Buy gifts at the gas station.

Moon.

Watch VH1 or the Cartoon Network more than 3 hours a week.

Wear colored contact lenses.

Recommend the cheapest thing on the menu when he's treating.

Smoke cloves.

Smoke "socially."

Wear camos to work
(unless he's in the
military).

**Complain to his friends
about his girlfriend's
physical shortcomings.**

Serve an elaborate dinner
on paper plates.

things a man
SHOULD NOT WEAR

Spats.

Diagonal stripes.

Flower prints.

Sandals (unless on a beach sporting a flower print, in which case his name is most certainly Jimmy Buffet).

Anything boasting the hue of a canary or banana (unless it's a Porsche).

A cell phone on a belt clip.

A cell phone on a belt clip with a blue-tooth earpiece and a beleagured assistant on the other end of the line.

A tie that hangs well below the beltline or glaringly above it.

A novelty tie, no matter how perfectly it hangs.

SHOULD NOT WEAR

A cheap suit.

A cheap suit with gold buttons.

Any item of clothing altered with a pair of scissors.

More jewelry than a wedding ring and a wristwatch.

A logo on the chest without a signed endorsement check in the pocket.

A hairstyle that demands of him more than sixty seconds.

Leather pants.

A prostitute.

Too much black (he doesn't want people thinking he's French).

His lady's scent, unless it rubbed off during rigorous physical activity.

Hit on the waitress when out on a date.

Join Friendster.

Yell, "Let's get naked!"

Ecstasy.

Allow his mother to buy his clothing.

Wear a tuxedo with Converse All-Stars.

Wear a T-shirt with a tuxedo printed on it.

Eat any food on a dare.

Pierce *anything*.

Steal magazines from
his dentist's office.

Show up at a party
empty-handed.

**Organize his record
collection by anything other
than alphabetical order.**

Be proud of
himself for
reading the paper.

Have a favorite Hilton sister.

Propose marriage
via stadium Jumbotron.

Decide anything of importance based on the ruminations of Howard Stern.

Grow a ponytail.

Subject someone other than his shrink to a scene-by-scene description of a dream he had.

Titter when someone says *pianist*.

Titter when someone says *titter*.

Find life lessons in *The Fountainhead* or *Atlas Shrugged*.

Write his name in
the snow with urine.

Laugh at David Spade,
even a little bit.

**Call "shotgun" before
getting in the car.**

Refute someone else's call of "shotgun."

Visit the restroom in
groups of three or more.

Refer to her lover as "Boo."

**Give out a fake name and
phone number at parties.**

Grovel in front of
a bouncer.

Shave her pubic hair in the shape of
a heart as a Valentine's Day gift.

Have sex with someone while another person is in the room (unless, of course, they are a participant).

Debate what sexual behavior qualifies as "hooking up."

Use a sick day to mourn the break up of her three-week relationship.

Ask the man she's dating which of her friends he would most like to sleep with.

Ask the man she's dating which of her body parts is the least desirable.

Get upset when he has an answer for either of the above.

Rap along with gender-derisive choruses like "Bitches ain't shit but hoes and tricks."

Get offended by such lyrics.

Read or quote any of the following books: *Why Men Love Bitches*; *Our Bodies, Ourselves*; *He's Just Not That Into You*; *The Seat of the Soul*.

Ask for a raise in her allowance.

Audition for any show on MTV.

Create a "party" line, in which she and a friend call someone on three-way and she calls someone else and then she calls someone else, ad infinitum.

Replay a voicemail (for herself or her friends) more than twice.

Wear a baby T-shirt that reads, "Princess," or "Property Of _____."

Pinky swear.

Leave someone more than one unreturned voicemail a day.

Announce, "You're It," when she returns that person's call.

Greet men by punching them in the stomach and saying "What's up, Dude?"

Tivo *Powergirls.*

Use any word rhyming with -ing, -ang, or -ong when referring to male genitalia.

Practice the "Baby One More Time" choreography in her bedroom mirror.

Order White Zin.

Display her thong above her jeans.

Hostess, especially at a TGI Fridays, Chili's, or local strip club.

Dye any part of her hair a primary color.

Delay adhering to any of this advice for another ten years because "40 is the new 30."

Surreptitiously take the quizzes in women's magazines..

Attempt to cut his own hair.

Whine.

Mist up during Aerosmith's "Dream On."

Change plans because of a TV show.

Forget his wedding anniversary.

Forget his mother's birthday.

Forget where he came from and who he is.

Actually care which was better, *Star Trek* or *Star Trek: The Next Generation*.

Call his small social group by any nickname, especially "the wolf pack."

Wear a wallet with a chain.

Write anything on
a bathroom wall.

**Ask what the hourly
rate is at a hotel.**

Drive a Miata.

Teach his parrot curse words.

Believe he can
still make the NBA.

Seventeen year-olds,
even if they look 21.

Play more than an hour of video games a day.

Give someone a wedgie.

Intentionally sing poorly at karaoke.

Buy fireworks.

Brag about his "mad hockey skillz."

Drink Jagermeister.

Pay to see someone fuck a
donkey in Tijuana.

Fuck a donkey in Tijuana.

Sulk.

Toilet paper a house.

Buy a video game as a gift
for his girlfriend.

Ride a pony.

Listen to Dave
Matthews, Ben Harper
or Jack Johnson.
For the love of God!

things a man **SHOULD NEVER DO**
AFTER THE AGE OF ONE

Get circumcised.

Spend more than ten minutes looking at a checkerboard pattern (Exception: Peyote users).

Look longingly at his mother's breasts.

Urinate in his mouth.

Be terrified of Mr. Noodles on Elmo.

Cry uncontrollably at the sight of a wooden spoon.

Eat pureed Wheat Thins.

things a man **SHOULD NEVER DO**
AFTER THE AGE OF **ONE**

Suck on the corner of a laptop.

Go willingly into the arms of strangers.

Lose neck control.

Have a favorite Higglytown Hero.

"Make nice."

Wear a piece of clothing that resembles a unitard.

Read The Fountainhead.

By Jasper Jacobs
Age 14 months

Order the cookies at McDonald's.

Hit thirteen against a six.

Cannonballs.

Sign a document
without reading it.

Use a fake name
to get into a party.

Kill a pet from lack of feeding it.

Organize a party bus.

Drink wine from a box.

Hit on the baby sitter,
unless she is extremely hot.

Refer to returning a business associate's
phone call as "hitting you back."

Use his little finger and thumb as a fake telephone when telling a story that involves a phone call.

Play the "Stairway to Heaven" intro instead of just saying, "I don't play the guitar."

Smell his fingers . . . after anything.

Forward chain-letter emails.

Talk about his best Counter Strike score at a cocktail party.

Subscribe to *Maxim*.

Wear any sort of track suit, especially those made of velour or by Sergio Tacchini.

Shout "two points" every time he throws something in the trash from more than a yard away.

Buy a novelty postcard in another country with topless women on the beach and write "wish you were here" on it.

Bring his dirty laundry along when popping in to visit mom.

Get a tattoo with some kind of cartoon or comic book character, or, worse, of barbed wire.

Serve a dinner to friends using anything made by Kraft.

Wear a baseball cap backwards, sideways, or slightly off-center.

Lightly bang fists when a handshake will suffice.

Use numbers in place of words or locations, such as "the 411" for information.

Keg Stands.

Dress up as Britney, Jessica, or any of the Charlie's Angels for Halloween.

Begin a page in her journal "Dear Diary."

Watch any of the following more than twice a year: *Pretty Woman, Dirty Dancing, Love Actually, When Harry Met Sally, Ghost, Say Anything, Waiting to Exhale, Bridget Jones's Diary, The Princess Bride, Beaches, My Best Friend's Wedding.*

Refer to her promiscuous friend as "the Samantha of the group."

Refer to the elderly as "cute."

Only have sex with
the lights off.

Only have sex with other people.

End a disagreement
with "What-ever."

Use "so" for extra emphasis before an adjective.

Do that annoying thing, where she's constantly pulling her hair behind her ears, twisting it around her fingers, and tugging on it for no reason.

Forge her daddy's signature on a credit card receipt.

Only order drinks that taste like Kool-Aid.

Dance in a group of four or more women unless she's
a) in a half time show or
b) it's to "Hava Nagilah."

Wear non-prescription glasses for that "hot librarian look."

Put off learning how to read a map.

Practice writing her first name with the last name of someone whom she's known for less than six months.

Enter a wet T-shirt contest.

Yank another woman's hair, bra strap, or hoop earrings.

Pretend she's drunker than she is.

Buy any sartorial item that costs 15 percent of her monthly salary.

List the names of her prospective bridesmaids unless she will become an actual bride in a year's time, with the ring and the cashed check from the down payment for the reception to prove it.

Penny Wrenn

Pay more for designer clothing because it has been pre-ripped, pre-stained, or otherwise pre-damaged.

Wear two different colored Chuck Taylor high-tops.

Steal bowling shoes.

Use two different types of styling gel simultaneously.

Drink good liquor out of a plastic cup.

Plan a nationwide tour
of breweries.

Carry an expensive camera
that he doesn't know how
to use.

Own a pit bull.

Hang a hammock-chair.

Do the John Travolta point-to-the-ceiling-point-to-the-floor dance move; also that one from *Pulp Fiction*.

Collect anything that McDonald's gives out during a promotion.

Put less than $5 worth of gas into the tank.

Pour a beer for someone so that there's more than an inch of foam in the glass.

**Use the phrase "pole smoking"
to refer to kissing up.**

Keep a miniscule amount
of marijuana extremely
well hidden.

Announce to people at the party
how many drinks he's had so far.

**Order at Taco Bell using a slightly
Mexican accent.**

Use discarded wine bottles as
candle holders.

things a man over 30
SHOULD NOT READ

The novelization of *The Chronicles of Riddick.*

Decircumcision: Foreskin Restoration, Methods and Circumcision Practices.

Chain e-mails.

Horoscopes.

The Art of Auto Fellatio: Oral Sex for One.

Canadian Homes and Cottages magazine.

Evite RSVP responses.

Anything by Terry McMillan.

Us Weekly, or *In Touch*.

The escort pages in the phone book.

His father's porn collection.

Gawker.

On the Road.

Eat any meal that comes with plastic prizes.

Go to a monster truck rally.

Drink Boone's Farm, Natty Ice, or any cocktail mixed with 151.

Not vote.

Start a garage band.

Watch the *Dark Side of the Moon* laser light show at a planetarium.

Refer to your girlfriend's breasts as "The Twins."

Whippits.

Keep a weekly schedule of his neighborhood bar's weekly drink specials on his fridge.

things a man past the age of 30
SHOULD NOT **GOOGLE**

Lake Havusu Spring Break deals.

Portugal's hottest MILFs.

Ultimate Fighting registration.

Navy SEAL enlistment.

Motocross lessons.

Treatment + "Burning urination."

Roofies untraceable.

Akron rave scene.

Legends backyard wrestling.

Ultimate Frisbee official league rules.

Matrix trilogy metaphors.

Grand Theft Auto cheat codes.

Daphne from Scooby-Doo XXX pics.

Barking dog Jingle Bells downloads.

"Vagina."

Sum 41 Fan Club.

His ex-girlfriends.

Himself.

Dine and dash.

Sneak alcohol into a movie theater.

Buy his ties in bulk.

Say good-bye to anyone by tapping his chest and even so much as whispering "peace out."

Brag about how much Wasabi he can eat.

Smoke pot out of a soda can or cored apple.

Watch *SpongeBob SquarePants* after smoking said pot.

Wear fleece to the office.

Take literally the advice given to him by some book suggesting he's too old to do dumb stuff.

index